The  Of Humility: A Treatise
By
Pope Leo XIII

Translated by

Dom Joseph Jerome Vaughan, O.S.B.

With the permission of His Holiness

"He will save the humble of spirit" Ps. 33:19

St Athanasius Press
All Rights Reserved 2018

ISBN-13: 978-1721943722

ISBN-10: 1721943722

St Athanasius Press
All Rights Reserved 2018

Specializing in Reprinting
Catholic Classics!

CONTENTS

Preface of Translator 5

Joachim Cardinal Pecci 9

Prologue 12

The Practice of Humility 14

Sermon of St Augustine 63
On the Fear of God and on True Humility

Prayer 82
To implore the grace of devotion and of humility.

Discite a Me quia mitis sum et humilis corde.

"Learn of Me, because I am meek and humble of heart." Matt 11:29

Humilibus dat gratiam

"To the humble he giveth grace." 1 Peter 5:5

PREFACE OF TRANSLATOR

CARDINAL NEWMAN, when speaking in the Birmingham Oratory last January, on the occasion of the Papal Jubilee, said: "The Holy Father lived a long life before he became Pope, and little was known of him, yet he has now in the few years that he has become Pope done things which it may be said no other man could do. I scarcely sup pose that any of you here present had heard his name before he was made Pope. There did not seem any likelihood that he would ever leave Perugia, his bishopric, but he was found — as others have been found — by a special providence and inspiration of God, and we in our ignorance knew nothing of him."

This golden treatise on The Practice of Humility, from the pen of the reigning Sovereign Pontiff, now presented to the English public, comes then as a revelation, and lifts the veil which hitherto has concealed from view the long years of his comparative seclusion spent in Perugia. It shows us the work divine grace was achieving in his heart during that time of his "hidden life" of unconscious preparation for the tiara, and teaches us the school in which his grand character and lofty genius were formed and mellowed. Whilst delineating the humility which those aspiring to perfection should aim at, it in reality presents us with a beautiful portrait of the Holy Father himself, and brings us in touch with his very spirit. For to use the words which St Gregory the Great wrote of St Benedict: "So holy a man could by no means teach otherwise than as he lived" — Sandus vir nulio modo potuii aliter docere quam vixit.•

Those who have been compelled by duty to renounce the gratification of a pilgrimage to the Eternal City for the Papal Jubilee and to remain at home — those thousands of loyal sons and daughters of holy Mother Church scattered up and down the United Kingdom, in town and hamlet, in the noble house and the humble cottage — one and all, in reading this little work, will acquire a more familiar and intimate acquaintance with the Supreme Pastor of their souls than they could possibly enjoy by merely gazing upon his face and hearing his voice. By it the reader will be drawn under the spell and fascination of his vigorous intellect and striking eloquence, and led to exclaim; — "Are not his words as a fire and as a hammer that breaketh the rock in pieces?"

Though dedicated to his Seminarists, the book will be found very suitable to all classes and conditions of men. Is there not reason to think it will even be so cherished by the faithful as to rank with the "Imitation" and the "Spiritual Combat?" So true to life are its admonitions, so profound and searching its lessons, that throughout the Holy Father seems to speak as the spiritual director of every individual soul, as the physician of each human heart, and as the Good Shepherd seeking out the lost sheep. That one so well versed in the secrets of the interior life, and so fully acquainted with the sufferings of poor humanity, should place his finger upon "the Practice of Humility" as the crying want of the age, and as the most necessary exercise towards the formation of an ascetic priesthood, is not unnatural. For as our blessed Lord by His cross and by His humility drew all men unto Himself, so by the use of these same potent means will His Vicegerents upon earth ever continue to fulfil their glorious and divine mission in the world.

To those outside the fold, who, recognising the versatility and grasp of his master mind, have been hitherto accustomed to regard him merely as the finished scholar, and the acute philosopher, the great statesman and the arbiter of the nations, this book will reveal the secret which raised him to his present matchless glory — and withal that sustains him in it.

No thoughtful Christian will doubt that the true and supernatural explanation of all those achievements and triumphs may be traced to his humility of spirit. In fact, the Sovereign Pontiff pointed out this truth himself in those memorable, and, as it were, prophetic words spoken in reply to the address of the Sacred College on the day of his coronation, March 3rd, 1878: — "Convinced that the most merciful God is He Who chooses the weak things of this world to confound the strong, We live in the certainty that He will sustain Our weakness, and raise up Our lowliness in order to show forth His power and make His strength to shine."

In conclusion. His Holiness has embellished this treatise with a rich appendix of various thoughts culled from spiritual writers, and preceded by the sermon of the great Bishop of Hippo upon the "Fear of God and True Humility." On confronting in their originals St Benedict's immortal chapter on Humility with the discourse of St. Augustine, it is quite perceptible that this must have been a source from which the Monastic Legislator drew his inspirations, using as he does in one place its very words and expressions. It may be interesting to know that fourteen hundred years later, another Light and Lawgiver of the Church repaired to the same fountain. For at the audience in which the Pope graciously accorded permission for the present translation, he condescended to enter upon the motives which led him to compose this valuable treatise, avowing that it was this very sermon of St. Augustine which had inspired him with its first conception.

Joseph Jerome Vaughan, O.S.B.
Monte Cassino,
Whitsuntide, 1888

JOACHIM CARDINAL PECCI,
Bishop of Perugia.

To his most beloved Sons, the Seminarists.

THE foundation of Christian perfection, according to the common teaching of the holy fathers, is humility. "In order to become great," says St. Augustine, "it is necessary to begin by being little. You are desirous of building up the edifice of Christina virtues: know ye then that it is of an immense height. Endeavour, therefore, at once to lay its foundations very deep in humility; for he who is about to erect a building, first of all digs out the foundations in proportion to the bulk and height of the intended structure." (Ser. S. Aug. x. de Ver. Dom.)

Now this little treatise, which We dedicate to you, O dearly beloved sons, teaches you THE PRACTICE OF HUMILITY; that is, it teaches you to lay the foundations of Christian perfection. Think, then, of what great importance it must be to you who are bound to observe in a special manner that commandment of Jesus Christ, be ye perfect as your heavenly Father is perfect For this reason We feel sure that We are making you a gift which will prove exceedingly dear to you, not only from its being a fresh token of the love We bear you, but also because it will be a most efficacious means towards the salvation of your souls — that most important of all the works in which you may be engaged.

Also another motive has induced Us to address this little book to you: namely, the object of the ecclesiastical state which you have embraced. This object does not merely include your own sanctification, but also the promotion of that of others, by enlarging the kingdom of Jesus Christ through those very same means which He made use of when on earth, for humility of heart was His distinctive characteristic.

This same means will enable you to subdue the pride of the world, and to implant in the hearts of all men the mortification and the humility of the cross. Since Jesus Christ did not teach until He had first practised, you also, following His example, should enter upon the sacred ministry already well grounded in The Practice of Humility. From this interior and inexhaustible fountain of all virtues will flow forth words of comfort, encouragement, and zeal, whereby to establish the just in sanctity, and to recall those who have gone astray from the paths of vice and perdition into those of virtue and salvation.

Let each one of you in particular, then, be that scholar, who in this little treatise which We dedicate to you, imagines himself to be receiving from his spiritual master lessons on The Practice of Humility, and always remember, dear sons, that there is no greater consolation you can give Us than that of seeing you humble, meek, and obedient. Trusting, then, that We shall always find you to be such, and in the ardent desire We have that you be so verily and indeed, We bless you all in the Lord, not, however, without once more earnestly exhorting you to use every endeavour to carry out all that this little treatise shall counsel you to practise.

The Practice of Humility

Prologue

IT is an incontrovertible truth that the proud will meet with no mercy: that the gates of the kingdom of heaven will be closed against them, and that the Lord will open those gates to none but the Humble, To be convinced of this we need simply to open Holy Scripture. There we are taught in every page, that God resists the proud; that He humbles those who exalt themselves; that we must become like unto little children if we would enter into His glory; that we shall be excluded from it unless we bear this resemblance: in fine, that God pours forth His graces upon none but the humble.

Such being the case we cannot be too strongly impressed of what importance it is for all Christians, and more especially for those who embrace the ecclesiastical state, to endeavour to practise humility, and banish from their minds all presumption, all vanity, all pride.

To secure success in a work so holy no effort or labour should be spared; and as this cannot be attained without the grace of God, we must ask it of Him earnestly and very frequently.

Every Christian has contracted in holy Baptism

the obligation of walking in the footsteps of Jesus Christ. He is the divine Model to which we should conform our lives. Now in order to humble exaltation and heal the wound of our pride, our Blessed Redeemer carried humility to such a degree as to become the reproach of the world, thereby teaching us through His own example the one road that leads to heaven. The most important lesson taught us by our Saviour is, strictly speaking, this:
Learn of Me, Discite a Me.

Therefore, O disciple of this divine Master, if thou wouldst secure this most precious pearl, than which there is no surer pledge of sanctity or more certain token of predestination, receive with docility the counsels which I give thee, and faithfully carry them out into practice.

The Practice of Humility

I.

OPEN the eyes of thy soul and consider that of thine own thou hast nothing that is good wherewith to pride thyself upon being something.

Of thine own thou hast nothing but sin, weakness, and misery, and with regard to those gifts of nature and of grace which thou enjoyest, as thou hast received them from God, Who is the principle of thy being, so to Him alone is their glory due.

II.

Therefore, be deeply imbued with the idea of thine own nothingness, endeavouring to increase it continually in thy heart, in spite and to the shame of the pride that lords it over thee.

Be intimately persuaded that there is nothing in the world so utterly vain and ridiculous as to wish to be highly esteemed on account of certain endowments which thou hast received merely as a loan from the gratuitous bounty of the Creator: for as the Apostle says: "If thou hast received them, why dost thou glory as though they were thine, and as if thou hadst not received them." (1 Cor 4:7)

III.

Frequently ponder upon thy weakness, thy blindness, thy vileness, thy hard-heartedness, thy inconsistency, thy sensuality, thy insensibility towards God, thy attachment to creatures, and upon a host of other vicious inclinations that spring from thy corrupt nature.

Let this be to thee a strong motive for continually diving deeper into thine own nothingness, and for always appearing utterly small and vile in thine own eyes.

IV.

Let the recollection of the sins of thy past life remain ever imprinted on thy mind.

Above all things be thoroughly convinced that the sin of pride is an evil so abominable, that any other, be it on the earth above, or in hell beneath, is as nothing in comparison.

This was the sin which made the angels in heaven prevaricate, and that cast them headlong into hell; this it was that corrupted the whole human race and brought upon the earth an infinitude of evils, which will endure as long as the world endures, or rather as long as eternity.

Besides, a soul laden with sin is only worthy of hatred, contempt, and punishment. Imagine, therefore, what possible kind of esteem thou canst have of thyself — thou who hast already been guilty of so many sins. *But what the grace of God; His mercy + forgiveness bestow on you.* V

Consider, moreover, that there is no crime, however enormous or deplorable it may be, to which thy corrupt nature does not incline, and of which thou mayest not become guilty, and that it is only through the mercy of God, and the help of His grace, that thou hast been preserved from it up to the present, according to that saying of St. Augustine, "There is no sin in the world which one man has fallen into, which another may not commit, should the hand which created man fail to uphold him." (Solil c.15)

Weep in thy heart over so deplorable a state, and firmly resolve to reckon thyself one of the most unworthy of sinners.

VI.

Reflect frequently that thou must sooner or later die, and that thy body will have to rot in the grave.

Keep constantly before thine eyes the inexorable judgment seat of Jesus Christ, whither we must all necessarily appear.

Meditate upon the eternal torments of hell, prepared for the wicked, and more especially for those who are most like unto Satan — the proud.

Ponder seriously how, owing to the impenetrable veil that conceals the divine judgments from mortal eye, thou art absolutely uncertain whether or not thou wilt be of the number of those reprobates who, in the society of demons, will be cast for ever into that place of woe to be the undying victims of a fire enkindled by the very breath of the divine wrath.

This uncertainty should be of itself enough to keep thee in a state of the utmost humility, and inspire thee with a salutary fear.

VII.

Do not flatter thyself that thou wilt ever be able to acquire humility, unless thou dost practise those particular exercises which are conducive to it.

Acts of meekness, for instance, of patience, of obedience, of mortification, of self-hatred, of the renunciation of thine own feelings and opinions, of sorrow for thy sins, and the like.

Because these are the only weapons which will destroy in thee the earth of self-love, that abominable soil which germinates all thy vices, and wherein thy pride and presumption take root and spread out in luxuriant growth.

VIII.

As far as thou art able, preserve silence and recollection, but at all times endeavour to do so without inconveniencing others.

When thou art obliged to speak, always do so with reserve, and with modesty and simplicity.

And should it happen that no attention be paid to thee, whether out of contempt or from any other cause, do not show any resentment, but accept the humiliation, and bear it with resignation and tranquillity.

IX.

Most diligently guard against and carefully avoid giving utterance to disdainful and haughty expressions, displaying an assumption of superiority, as well as to all studied phrases, and every kind of frivolous jest.

Be ever silent on such matters as might lead others to believe thee to be clever and intellectual, and well worthy of their esteem. In a word, never talk of thyself without good reason, nor desire to speak of things calculated to bring upon thee honour and praise.

X.

In thy conversation abstain from such observations and sarcastic remarks as may give pain to others; in a word, avoid all that savours of the spirit of the world.

Seldom speak of spiritual matters in a magisterial tone or as one giving advice, unless thy charge or charity obliges thee to do so.

Speak only of these things in order to be instructed by one who understands such matters, and whom thou knowest to be capable of giving thee seasonable advice; for to pose as a master in things spiritual without necessity, is to add fuel to the burning fire — that is to one's soul, which is already ablaze with pride.

XI.

Repress to the best of thy ability all vain and useless curiosity, and be not over-anxious to see what worldlings call things of rarity, beauty, and splendour.

Study rather to know thy duty, and what is conducive to thy perfection and salvation.

XII.

Be always very exact and attentive in treating thy superiors with the greatest respect and reverence, thy equals with esteem and courtesy, and thy inferiors with charity.

Take it for granted that any other behaviour is the sure sign of a soul ruled by pride.

XIII.

Following the maxims of the Holy Gospel, always seek the lowest place, thoroughly convinced that such is precisely what befits thee.

So also, in all the requirements of life, beware lest thy desires and cares should embrace too much and aspire too high.

Be satisfied rather with simple and humble things, as being better suited to thine own littleness.

XIV.

If earthly consolations fail thee, and if God withdraw all spiritual sweetnesses, remember that thou hast ever abundantly enjoyed them beyond thy deserts, and rest satisfied with the way in which the Lord deals with thee.

XV.

Cultivate unceasingly within thy soul the pious custom of accusing, reproaching, and condemning thyself.

Judge all thine own actions severely, being as they truly are nearly always accompanied with a thousand defects and with the continual arrogance of self-love.

Often conceive a just contempt of thyself, seeing how much thou art wanting in prudence, simplicity, and purity of heart in all thy actions.

XVI.

Beware, as of a most grievous evil, of condemning the actions of others, but interpret their every word and deed leniently, seeking with industrious charity for reasons to excuse and defend them.

Should the fault committed be so evident as to allow no opening for defence, strive to attenuate it as far as may be, attributing it to inattention, surprise, or to some such similar cause, according to circumstances.

At all events, think no more of it, unless by reason of thy office thou art obliged to apply a remedy.

XVII.

Never contradict anyone in conversation, when the point under discussion is an open question, and when there is as much to be said for it as against.

Do not get over-excited in arguing, but if thy opinion be considered erroneous or of little worth, give way quietly and then humbly remain silent.

Yield also and behave in like manner with respect to matters of no consequence even when thou art satisfied of the mistake of that which has been asserted.

On all other occasions when it is of importance to defend the truth, do so courageously, but without being violent or contemptuous.

Rest assured that thou wilt more likely win by gentleness than by thy impetuosity and resentment.

XVIII.

Be well on thy guard against giving pain, either by word, action, or in thy manner to anyone, however much he may be beneath thee, unless thou shouldst be at times constrained to do so by duty, obedience, or charity.

XIX.

Should there be anyone who is continually coming in and out, and pestering thee, and making it his business on every occasion to insult thee with outrage and injury, yield not to feelings of anger, but look upon him as an instrument which God in His mercy makes use of for thy good, so as to heal the inveterate wound of thy pride.

XX.

The passion of anger, which derives its violence from that very pride wherein it is rooted, is a vice not to be tolerated in anyone, much less in religious persons.

Endeavour, therefore, to lay up a good store of gentleness, so that should anyone insult thee, and wound thy feelings with injuries, be they never so grievous, thou mayest still have strength enough to retain thy equanimity.

And take great care lest in such cases thou nourish or harbour in thy heart feelings of dislike and revenge against the person who hath offended thee; yea, rather forgive him from thy heart, being convinced that thou canst have no better disposition than this for obtaining pardon of those injuries which thou hast committed even against God Himself.

Be assured that such humble forbearance will earn for thee an abundant harvest of merit in heaven.

XXI.

Be kindly and patient in bearing with the defects and weaknesses of others, keeping always before thine eyes thine own miseries, by reason of which thou also art in need of being borne with and compassionated by others.

XXII.

In a word, show humility and meekness towards all, but more especially towards those for whom thou feelest some repugnance and aversion, avoiding the exclamation which some persons make: — "God forbid that I should entertain any hatred against that man, but I cannot abide his being near me, nor do I care to have anything at all to do with him."

Take it for granted that this dislike arises also from pride, and from thy not having conquered haughty nature and self-love with the weapons of grace.

For if these persons would truly abandon themselves to the inspirations of divine grace, they would very soon feel all the difficulties which they experience within themselves overcome by a true humility, and would patiently bear with natures which are even rougher and more uncongenial.

XXIII.

Should any affliction overtake thee, bless the Lord, Who hath so ordained it for thy greater good.

Believe that thou hast deserved it, and even more and greater troubles, and art not worthy of any consolation.

Thou mayest ask the Lord in all simplicity to deliver thee from it, if such be pleasing unto Him, otherwise beg Him to give thee strength to bear thy trial meritoriously.

In thy crosses seek not for exterior consolation, especially when it is evident that God sends them to thee for thy humiliation, and to abate thy pride and presumption, but exclaim with the royal Psalmist: — "It is good for me, O Lord, that Thou hast humbled me, that I may learn Thy Justifications" Ps. 118:71

XXIV.

For the same reason yield not to feelings of annoyance and disgust at table, because the food set before thee is little suited to thy taste.

Do in this case as the poor of Jesus Christ, who willingly eat whatever is set before them, giving thanks unto Providence.

XXV.

If anyone blame or speak ill of thee unjustly, or if thy conduct be censured by one who is either thy inferior, or who, being more deserving of reprehension than thyself, should look to his own shortcomings, I would not have thee on that account fly into a passion, or fling aside the counsels which I have given thee, and refuse to examine thy conduct in the light of God — and this, from the intimate persuasion that thou art liable to go astray at every step if the grace of the Lord did not preserve thee.

XXVI.

Never wish to be singularly loved: for as love depends upon the will, and as the will by its nature tends to that which is good, it follows that to be loved and to be considered good are one and the same thing.

But the desire of being considered exceptionally good, and being esteemed above others, cannot be reconciled with true humility.

O! What great fruit thou mightest derive from acting up to this doctrine!

For thy soul, yearning then no longer for the love of creatures, would hide itself in the sacred wounds of its Saviour.

There, in the adorable Heart of her Jesus, she would experience ineffable divine sweetness, because having generously renounced the love of creatures for His sake, she would be able to taste abundantly that honey of divine consolation, which would be denied her were she taken up with the false and deceitful sweetnesses of earthly consolations.

For divine consolation is so pure and real that it will not suffer the admixture of that which is earthly; and we are replenished with the one in proportion as we feel disgust for the other.

Moreover, thy soul will be able to turn herself freely to God, and by the thought of His presence and infinite perfections to abide in His enjoyment.

Finally, as there is nothing more delightful than to love and be loved, so if thou deprivest thyself of this pleasure for the love of God, and in order that He may possess thy heart whole and undivided, thou offerest a most acceptable sacrifice to God, and one that is in the highest degree meritorious.

Nor fear lest by so doing thy love for thy neighbour should grow cold; yea thou wilt rather love him with a purer and more perfect love, loving him no longer out of self-interest, that is for the gratification of thy own inclinations, but purely for the sake of pleasing God, and of doing that which thou knowest to be acceptable to Him.

XXVII.

Perform all thine actions, be they never so trifling, with great attention and the utmost exactness and diligence, because doing them thoughtlessly and hastily is the result of presumption.

The truly humble man is always upon his guard, fearing lest there should be something amiss even in his smallest actions.

For the same reason thou shouldst always prefer to practise ordinary exercises of piety, and shun in general all such extraordinary things as thine own inclination may suggest to thee.

For as the proud man always seeks to make himself singular, so the humble man finds his delight in practices which are common and ordinary.

XXVIII.

Know that thou art not fit to be thine own counsellor, and therefore shouldst fear and be diffident of thine own opinions as proceeding from a source that is marred and corrupt.

Under this conviction thou wilt, as far as it is possible, always take counsel of some wise and conscientious person, and prefer rather to be led by one better than thyself than to follow thine own devices.

XXIX.

Whatever high degree of grace and virtue thou hast attained; whatever gift of prayer God hath bestowed upon thee, let it be as sublime as thou wilt; even if thy life hath been one of a thousand years spent in innocence and fervour of devotion — thou oughtest, nevertheless, to walk always in fear and self-distrust, and more especially in matters touching purity.

Recollect that thou carryest about in thee an indestructible germ and an inexhaustible fountain of sin, and know that thou art all weakness, all unstableness, all unfaithfulness.

Look, therefore, always to thyself: close thine eyes and ears so as neither to see nor hear anything that might sully thy soul.

Always shun dangerous occasions, and with the other sex avoid all useless conversations, and in those that are necessary, maintain the most scrupulous modesty and reserve.

Lastly, as thou canst do nothing good without the grace of God, beg of Him constantly to have mercy on thee, and not for a single instant to leave thee to thyself

XXX.

Hast thou perchance received great talents from God, or art thou perhaps famous in the world for some great achievement? Then do thou, for this very reason, endeavour the more to know thyself as thou truly art, and seek by careful introversion to convince thyself of thine own weakness, of thine own incapacity, and of thine own nothingness.

Thou oughtest to appear in thine own eyes less than a little child, and not to take delight in the praises of men, and to beware of being ambitious of honour: yea, rather thou shouldst always reject both the one and the other.

XXXI.

Shouldst thou sustain any grievous injury or meet with some keenly felt disappointment, instead of being indignant against him who hath offended thee, lift up thine eyes to heaven and fix them upon the Lord, Who in His infinite
and loving Providence hath so ordained it, either for the expiation of thy sins, or to destroy in thee the spirit of pride, reducing thee to practise acts of patience and humility.

XXXII.

When thou meetest with an opportunity of rendering thy neighbour some lowly and menial service, do so with joy, and with that humility which thou wouldst have wert thou the servant of all.

By this practice thou wilt lay up In store for thyself treasures of virtue and grace.

XXXIII.

Busy not thyself in the least about things which do not in any way concern thee, and of which thou art not called upon to give an account either to God or to man.

For meddling comes of secret pride and from vain

presumption; it nourishes and increases vanity, and begets an infinite host of troubles, worries, and distractions; whereas, by attending to one's self alone and to one's own duties, a man will find a fountain of peace and tranquillity, according to that beautiful saying of the "Imitation of Christ:" — "Neither busy thyself with things not committed to thy care, and thus may it be brought about that thou shalt be little or seldom disturbed." B. iii. ch. 25.

XXXIV.

When thou performest some extraordinary mortification, take good care to keep free from the venom of vain glory, which oftentimes mars the whole merit.

Take care, I say, to perform it for this sole reason — that it is not becoming in thee, since thou art so great a sinner, to live at thine own ease and pleasure, and because thou hast so many defects and debts to make satisfaction for in the sight of the divine justice.

Reflect that as the bit and bridle are necessary to master a mettlesome horse, so works of penance are necessary for thee in order to check the violence of thy passions and keep thee within the bounds of duty.

XXXV.

Every time thou art inclined to be impatient or downcast in thy tribulations and humiliations, courageously fight against such a temptation, being mindful of thy sins, for which thou hast deserved far severer chastisements than those from which thou art actually suffering.

Adore the infinite justice of God, and with reverence receive its blows, which thou shouldst regard as so many fountains of mercy and of grace.

Oh! If thou couldst but understand how salutary it is to be smitten in this miserable life by the hand of so sweet a Father as God is, thou wouldst then, without doubt, abandon thyself wholly and entirely into His hands.

Frequently cry out with St. Augustine: "Here in this life, O Lord, burn within me, and cut whatsoever Thou pleasest; here spare me not, provided Thou dost spare and pardon me in eternity."

To refuse tribulations is to rebel against the justice of God, which is so salutary; it is also to reject that chalice which He offers us in His mercy, and which Jesus Christ Himself, although innocent, desired to be the first to drink.

XXXVI.

If by any chance thou hast committed some fault which has caused thee to be despised by the person who witnessed it, conceive a lively sorrow for thy offence against God, and for the bad example given to thy neighbour; but, with regard to the contempt itself, and the dishonour incurred, accept them as a means which God has chosen for the expiation of thy fault, and to render thee more humble and more virtuous.

If, on the contrary, the seeing thyself depreciated and dishonoured mortifies and pains thee, believe me, thou dost not possess true humility, and art still infected with pride.

In this case, all the more earnestly implore the Lord to heal and save thee; for if God be not moved to pity towards thee, thou shalt certainly fall into other abysses.

XXXVII.

If amongst thy companions there be one who seemeth to thee contemptible and of no account, thou wilt act wisely and prudently in setting about to consider the good qualities of nature and of grace with which God has endowed him and on account of which he may appear worthy of respect and honour, rather than in noticing his faults and censuring them.

At least, always behold in him one created by God, formed after the divine image and likeness, and redeemed by the precious Blood of Jesus Christ; a Christian illuminated by the light of God's countenance, a soul capable of seeing and possessing God for all eternity, and perhaps one even predestined in the secret counsels of His adorable Providence.

And dost thou then know the graces which the Lord hath already poured out upon his heart, or is about to pour out upon it?

But without troubling thyself about such questions, it would perhaps be better to drive away immediately all those thoughts of contempt as the poisoned breath of the tempter.

XXXVIII.

When thou art praised, instead of rejoicing thereat, fear lest such praise be the sole reward of that little good which thou hast done.

In thy heart acknowledge thine own misery by which thou meritest the contempt of others, and endeavour to cut short that discourse; not indeed with a view of securing still greater praise — like the proud, who make a parade of humility — but with a holy adroitness, so that attention may be wholly drawn away from thee.

But if in this thou dost not succeed, instantly refer to God alone all the honour and all the glory, saying with Baruch and Daniel: — " To the Lord our God. belongeth justice, but to us confusion of our face." Bar 1:15

XXXIX.

As thine own praises should give thee disgust, so in the same degree ought the praises conferred upon others to cause thee delight: and do thou also contribute thy mete of praise so far as sincerity and truth will permit

The envious cannot endure the glory bestowed upon their neighbour, because they regard it as so much taken from their own.

For this very reason they adroitly let fall in their conversations certain half finished thoughts and ambiguous phrases, either to lessen or cast doubt on the praises which they hear conferred upon others.

Not thus shouldst thou act; but in praising thy neighbour praise and thank the Lord for the gifts He has bestowed upon him, and for the services which He receives at his hands.

XL.

When thy neighbour is defamed in thy hearing, conceive a sincere sorrow for it.

Seek in thy mind for some motive whereby to excuse the weakness of the detractor.

Do not fail, however, to defend the honour and good name of the poor person who is the object of attack, doing so with such skill and tact that the defence shall not turn out to be in reality a second accusation.

Thus, for example, at times try and touch upon his praiseworthy qualities, or put in a clear light how highly he is esteemed by others as well as by thyself; at times endeavour to change in a skilful way the subject of conversation, or let it be in some way understood how distasteful it is to thee.

By acting thus, thou wilt confer the utmost benefit upon thyself, the detractor, the bystanders, and the person maligned.

But if without making the slightest effort to repress thy feelings, thou dost feel pleased when thy neighbour is depreciated, and when he is extolled, displeased, O then, how much still remains for thee to do before possessing the incomparable treasure of humility.

XLI.

There is nothing more conducive to thy spiritual advancement than to be told of thy faults.

Hence it is very expedient and necessary that thou shouldst encourage those who sometimes have done thee this service that they may continue to do so on every occasion.

Since thou hast received their admonitions with joy and gratitude, make it thy duty to put them into practice, and this, not only because of the advantage which self-correction brings with it, but also in order to show to these faithful friends that their care of thee has not been in vain, and that thou art extremely sensible of their kindness.

The proud man, even when he corrects himself, does not wish it to appear that he is following the salutary counsels which he has received of others; nay, he even shows a supreme contempt for them.

But the truly humble man glories in submitting himself to all persons for the love of God, and looks upon the wise admonitions he receives as coming from God Himself, without reflecting upon the instrument which is made use of.

XLII.

Abandon thyself entirely to God in order to follow the dispensations of His loving Providence, even as a tender child casts itself without reserve into the arms of its beloved father.

Let God do with thee whatsoever He pleases, without disturbing or disquieting thyself about anything that may befall thee.

With joyfulness, with confidence, and with reverence, accept everything that comes to thee from Him.

To act otherwise, would be to requite the goodness of His heart with ingratitude — would be to distrust Him!

Humility plunges us infinitely below the infinite Being of God, but at the same time it teaches us that in Him alone is all our strength and every consolation.

XLIII.

Since it is clear that with out God thou art not able to do any good whatsoever, and that thou wouldst fall at every step and be overcome by the slightest temptation, always acknowledge thyself to be the weak and impotent creature thou art, bearing in mind that in all thy actions, thou standest continually in need of the divine assistance.

By means of these thoughts keep thyself inseparably united to God, even as the infant clings to the bosom of its mother, knowing of no other secure support

Say often with the royal Prophet: — "Unless the Lord had been my helper, my soul had almost dwelt in hell" Ps. 93:17 And: — "Look Thou upon me and have mercy on me, for I am alone and poor." Ps. 24:16 And: — "O God, come to my assistance; O Lord, make haste to help me" Ps. 69:1

Lastly, cease not to give thanks to the Lord with all the outpouring of thy heart. Above all things, thank Him for the protection with which He forestalls and encompasses thee.

Beg Him constantly to deign to give thee those special helps of which thou standest in need, and which He alone is able to bestow.

XLIV.

In the hour of prayer, more especially than at any other time, thou shouldst be penetrated with a feeling of shame and confusion and self-abasement, and with a holy awe of the presence of that Supreme Majesty to Whom thou dost dare appeal: — "I will speak to the Lord, whereas I am but dust and ashes." Gen. 17:27

If in thy prayer thou receivest some extraordinary favour, thou shouldst at once believe thyself to be unworthy of it, and understand that God has bestowed it upon thee gratuitously, and out of His pure mercy.

Guard thyself well against imagining that it belongs to thee of right, and against taking any vain complacency in it

And if thou dost not receive any such signal gift, thou shouldst not be on that account cast down.

Rather reflect that much yet remains for thee to do before thou art worthy of such favours, and that God is exceedingly good and patient even in permitting thee simply to lie at His feet, and to be, as it were, like the poor beggar, who waits whole hours at the door of the rich man's house, to obtain some trifling alms wherewith to alleviate his misery.

XLV.

Be ever most prompt in giving to God the entire glory both of thy good deeds and of the happy issue of the undertakings committed to thy care.

To thyself, attribute nothing except their defects,

for these emanate from thyself alone; whereas every good is from God, and to Him only are due the thanks and the glory of every good deed.

Impress this truth so deeply upon thy mind as never to forget it

Believe, that any other person helped by divine grace as thou hast been, would have succeeded far better than thou hast lone, and would not be guilty of so many imperfections.

Reject the praises which may be offered thee for any unexpected success, for they are not due to so vile an instrument as thou art; but rather to that immense, sublime, and eternal Master-Builder Who is able, if He hath a mind, to make use of a rod to strike water out of the rock, of a little clay to restore sight to the blind, and Who hath power to work an infinity of miracles.

XLVI.

If, on the contrary, the affairs placed under thy direction go wrong, it is much to be feared that the failure must be attributed to thy incapacity and to thy negligence.

Thy self-love and thy pride, which recoil from every humiliation, would seek perhaps to throw the blame upon others, and when unable to do this, would strive at least to extenuate the fault.

But do not encourage these vicious inclinations. Examine thy conduct conscientiously, and trembling lest thou hast failed in doing thy duty, acknowledge thy fault before God, and accept the humiliation as a chastisement which thou hast deserved.

If, however, thy conscience does not reproach thee, adore even in this case the dispensations of God, and reflect that perhaps thy past sins and too much self-confidence have caused the blessing of heaven to be withdrawn from thy labours.

XLVII.

When approaching the most holy Communion, with a heart all inflamed with divine love, thou shouldst at the same time approach with a mind penetrated with sentiments of true humility.

And how couldst thou not be wholly amazed on reflecting that a God, infinitely pure and infinitely holy, entertains such a surpassing degree of love for so miserable a creature as thou art, even to the giving thee His very Self for food!

Dive as deeply as thou canst into the abyss of thine unworthiness. Draw not nigh to that adorable Sanctity except with the utmost reverence.

And when it shall please that amiable Lord, Who in this Sacrament is all Love, to caress thee, communicating Himself to thee in the plenitude of His unutterable sweetness, take every possible precaution against falling away from the reverence due to His infinite majesty.

Keep thyself always in thy proper place that is, in submission, in subjection, and in thy nothingness.

And yet the sense of thy poverty and wretchedness ought not in any way to produce the effect of closing up thy heart, or of depriving thee in the least of that holy confidence which thou shouldst have in this heavenly Banquet.

Nay, it should make thee grow in love towards God, Who humbles Himself to such a degree as to become the nourishment of thy soul.

XLVIII.

For thy neighbour entertain true and living charity, and a perpetual fountain of affability and sweetness, and seek with a holy avidity how to help him in all things. But always do so to please God.

Examine well the motives of thy actions, and thus

thou shalt discover every snare of vanity and self-love.

Refer all the good thou dost to God alone.

Know that if thou keepest a good action so hidden and secret as to be known to none but God, it shall secure thee a priceless reward.

If, however, through thy negligence it becomes noised abroad, then, like a beautiful fruit which the birds have begun to peck at, it loses almost all its value.

XLIX.

Seeing thyself in continual danger of falling, let that wholesome fear which thou shouldst entertain of displeasing the Lord, be ever accompanied by an interior sigh towards Him, that His infinite mercy may preserve thee from so great a misfortune.

These interior sighs are, in reality, those groanings and yearnings of the heart recommended by the saints, which prompt us to attend to ourselves and to our own actions, to the meditation of divine truths, to the contempt of all things fleeting, to the practice of interior prayer, and to the keeping ourselves estranged from all that is not of God.

In a word, this practice is a fountain of true humility and poverty of spirit.

Make frequent use of it, and as far as in thee lies, let it be thy continual prayer.

L.

A sick man, who ardently desires to be cured, takes the greatest pains to ward off everything that might retard his progress, eats with the utmost moderation, even the most wholesome food, and considers at almost every mouthful whether it may or may not do him harm.

So, in like manner, if thou earnestly desirest to be cured of the fatal disease of pride, and if thou truly aspirest to the precious possession of humility, thou must be always attentive and cautious lest thou sayest or doest anything which might impede thee therein.

And with this object, it will be well on each occasion to ponder whether that which thou art about to do, tends or tends not to humility, in order either to do it immediately with joy or to discard it entirely.

LI.

Another exceedingly powerful motive to induce thee to practise the beautiful virtue of humility is the example of our Divine Saviour, Whom we should continually take as our Model.

He it is Who saith to us in the holy Gospel: — "Learn of Me^ because I am meek and humble of heart" Matt. 11:29.

And, in fact, as St Bernard remarks: "What pride is there which the humility of this divine Master cannot extinguish?"

Verily it may be said that He alone in reality humbles and abases Himself, and that we, when we seem to humiliate ourselves, do not lower ourselves at all, but simply take the place which belongs to us.

For being vile creatures, guilty perhaps of a thousand misdeeds, we can lay claim to no other right than nothingness and punishment.

But our Saviour Jesus Christ, lowered Himself infinitely beneath that lofty height which belongs to Him.

He is the omnipotent God, the infinite and immortal Being, the Supreme Arbiter of all things.

And notwithstanding this, He became man — weak, mortal, subject to suffering, obedient even unto death.

He has borne the lack of all temporal things. He Who in heaven constitutes the joy and the beatitude of the angels and of the saints, willed to become the "Man of Sorrows," and took upon Himself each and all of the miseries of humanity.

The uncreated Wisdom, and of all wisdom the Principle, has borne the shame and mockery due to a fool.

The Holy of Holies and Sanctity in essence, suffered Himself to be reputed a villain and a malefactor.

He Whom the countless hosts of the blessed in heaven adore, willed to die a disgraceful death upon a cross.

And lastly, He Who by nature is the Sovereign Good, has endured every kind of human misery.

Then, after such an example of humility, what ought we not to do — we who are but dust and ashes!

And what humiliation should ever appear hard to us — to us, who are not only most abject and vile worms, but what is worse still, most miserable sinners.

LII.

Consider, moreover, the examples left thee by the saints, both of the Old and the New Covenant. Isaias, that prophet so virtuous and zealous, believed himself to be impure in the sight of God, and openly declared that all his "justices" were as filthy "rags." Isaias 64:6.

Daniel, whom God Himself, in the Book of Ezechiel, describes as a holy man, capable of arresting by his prayers the divine wrath, spoke to God with the humility of a sinner, and as one who ought always to be overwhelmed with confusion and shame.

St. Dominic, a prodigy of innocence and holiness, had attained to such a degree of self-contempt, as to fear lest he should draw down the curse of heaven upon those cities through which he was obliged to pass.

Therefore, before entering them, he would prostrate with his face to the earth, and weeping, cry out: — "I conjure Thee, O my God, through Thy most tender mercy, to regard not my sins, lest this city, which is about to suffer me to linger within its walls, should in consequence feel the effects of Thy just vengeance."

St. Francis, who through his purity of life, merited to bear in his body the marks of the Passion of Jesus Christ, firmly and sincerely believed himself to be the most wicked of men.

This persuasion so possessed his mind that no one was ever able by any means to disabuse him of it.

The reason he gave for it was this: that if the least of mankind had received from God all those signal graces which had been bestowed upon him, such an one would have made far better use of them, and certainly would not have requited them with such base ingratitude.

Various other saints believed themselves unworthy of the food of which they partook, of the air they breathed, of the clothing which covered them.

Others looked upon it as an extraordinary miracle of the divine mercy that they were suffered to remain upon the face of the earth, and were not precipitated headlong into hell.

Others again wondered how their fellow-men could put up with them, and why the whole of creation did not unite as one man to exterminate and annihilate them.

Lastly, the saints have all held in abhorrence dignities, praises, and honours, and from that utmost contempt with which they regarded themselves, we see that they longed for naught else than humiliations and scorn.

And .art thou more illuminated or holier than they?

Why not then place, as did these saints, thy sole and entire delight in holy humility?

LIII.

Now to increase the more in this virtue and render humiliations sweet and familiar, thou wilt find it of great advantage to picture to thyself frequently the affronts which might come upon thee unawares, endeavouring, notwithstanding rebellious nature, to accept them as sure pledges of the love of thy God and as certain means for thine own sanctification.

Perhaps in doing this thou mayest have to undergo many struggles, but act courageously and be valiant in the strife, until thou feelest thyself firm and resolute to suffer all with joy for the love of Christ.

LIV.

Let not a day pass in which thou reproachest not thyself for that for which thy enemies might reproach thee; and that not only to sweeten beforehand the effect of such reproaches, but more especially to maintain thee in a state of lowliness and self-disesteem.

But if it should happen that in the tempest of some violent temptation thou art inclined to be impatient and to murmur interiorly at the way in which God tries thee, repress these feelings betimes, and say within thyself: — What! should a vile and miserable sinner such as I, dare complain of this tribulation?

And have I not already deserved punishments infinitely worse?

Knowest thou not, O my soul, that humiliations and sufferings are indeed thy true bread, bestowed upon thee as an alms by the Lord, so that thou mayest for once and all rise up out of thy misery and want?

Ah! Shouldst thou refuse these alms, thou art not worthy of them, rejecting as thou dost so rich a treasure, which perhaps will be taken away from thee and given to others to make better use of.

"The Lord wishes to number thee amongst His friends and disciples on Calvary, and wouldst thou, yielding to base fear, make the great refusal of combat?

(An allusion to Dante (Inferno iii. 60), where the poet vindictively attributes the abdication — "il gran rifuto" — of Celestine V. (1294) to cowardice, and in consequence places him in that circle of Hell inhabited by those distained alike by justice and mercy.)

"And how canst thou expect to be crowned without having fought? And how canst thou claim thy wages when thou hast not borne the burdens of the day and the heats?"

These and the like reflections will rekindle thy fervour, and will beget in thee a desire of leading a life, even of suffering and humiliation, in imitation of the life of our Saviour Jesus Christ.

LV.

However great may be the peace and tranquillity which thou enjoyest in the midst of abuse and contradiction, thou shouldst not on that account take it for granted that thou possessest a calm and triumphant humility, because pride is frequently only dormant, and if it happen to be aroused, it begins anew to inflict upon the soul serious injuries and losses.

Let the study of the knowledge of thyself, the fleeing from honours, and the love of humiliations, be thy weapons; and of these thou shouldst never divest thyself, nay, not even for a single moment.

If thus thou shalt acquire that rich inheritance of humility, then wilt thou have no longer any fear of losing it, because it is only by continually humbling thyself that thou shalt preserve the precious gift of humility.

LVI.

In order that God may deign to grant thee so great a favour, take for thy advocate and protectress the most blessed Virgin.

S. Bernard says that Mary, more than any other creature, humbled herself, and that being the greatest of all human beings, she, through the most profound abyss of her humility, made herself the least.

For this very reason Mary received the plenitude of grace, and became worthy to be the Mother of God.

At the same time, Mary is a Mother of mercy and tenderness, to whom no one ever has had recourse in vain.

Full of confidence, abandon thyself to her maternal heart. Beseech her to obtain for thee that virtue which was so dear to her. Fear not that she will be loath to take this petition under her special care.

No! Mary will demand it for thee from God, Who

quickens the humble and annihilates the proud.

Moreover, as Mary is all-powerful with her Son, He will certainly grant her request

Fly to her in all thy wants, in all thy temptations. Let Mary be thy support, let Mary be thy consolation.

But the chief grace which thou shouldst ask of her is holy humility. Do not hold thy peace, neither cease imploring until she has obtained it.

Nor fear being too importunate.

O! How pleasing to Mary is this importunity to obtain the salvation of thy soul, and to render thyself more acceptable to her Divine Son.

Lastly, that thou mayest induce her to be more and more favourable and propitious, conjure her by her own humility, which was the cause of her elevation to the dignity of Mother of God, and by her divine maternity, which was the ineffable fruit of her humility.

LVII.

For the same reason, thou shouldst also have recourse to those saints in whom this pre-eminent virtue has shone forth the most conspicuously.

For instance, to St. Michael the Archangel, who was the first of the humble, as Lucifer was the first of the proud.

To St. John the Baptist, who having attained to so sublime a degree of sanctity as to be taken for the Messias, nevertheless had so mean an opinion of himself that he thought he was unworthy even to loose the latchet of His shoes.

To St. Paul, that privileged Apostle, who was rapt up to the third heavens, and who, after having heard the inner-most secrets of the Divinity, regarded himself as the least of the Apostles, and even unworthy of the name of an Apostle, and to be, as it were, a mere nothing. 2 Cor 12:2

To St. Gregory, Pope, who took more pains to escape the Supreme Pontificate of the Church than the ambitious take to secure the highest honours.

To St. Augustine, who in the height of his fame, and extolled by all his contemporaries, both as a holy Bishop and as the most acute Doctor of the Catholic Church, left to the whole world in those two marvellous books of his — the "Confessions" and "Retractations" — immortal monuments of his humility.

To St. Alexius, who, within the walls of his paternal home, preferred the insults and ill-treatment of his very servants, to all the honours and dignities which he might so easily have obtained.

To St. Aloysius Gonzaga, who, lord and marquess of a vast estate, renounced it with joy, and in preference to a grand position in the world,, chose a life of humility and mortification.

In a word, thou shouldst have recourse to those other numerous saints, who by reason of their humility, shine with a most brilliant lustre in the annals of the Church.

Rest assured, that these humble servants of God will intercede for thee before His throne in heaven, that thou also mayest attain to being of the number of the faithful imitators of their virtue.

LVIII.

Lastly, the drawing nigh frequently to the sacraments of Penance and Communion, will supply most abundant aid to maintain thee in the practice of humility.

Confession, in which we reveal to a fellow-creature all the most secret and shameful miseries of our souls, is the greatest act of humiliation which Jesus Christ enjoined upon His disciples.

Holy Communion, by which we receive within our breasts in very substance the God made man and annihilated for love of us, is a wonderful school of humility and a most powerful means of acquiring it How canst thou doubt but that thine amiable Jesus desires to communicate this virtue of humility to thee when His Sacred Heart, that Heart so meek and humble, that furnace of love and charity, is reposing, as it were, upon thine own heart, and thy heart asks it of Him with all the fervour of its affections.

Approach as frequently as thou art able to receive this adorable Sacrament; and provided that thou dost bring unto It the necessary dispositions, thou shalt always find in It that hidden manna reserved for him only who seeks It with great eagerness.

LIX,

For the rest, always take courage in overcoming the difficulties thou shalt encounter in practising what I have taught thee thus far, and in resisting the opposition which thou shalt find within thyself

Be well on thy guard against exclaiming with the faint-hearted disciples: — "This is a hard sayings who can bear it?" John 6:61 — and who can carry it out into practice?

For of a truth I assure thee, that all the bitterness

thou shalt find at the outset, will very quickly be changed into ineffable sweetness and heavenly consolations.

A holy perseverance in these exercises will free thee from a thousand torments of soul, and will infuse into thy heart so much peace and tranquillity that thou shalt enjoy a foretaste of that eternal happiness which God hath prepared in heaven for His faithful servants.

If, through cowardice thou dost give up practising the necessary means to become truly humble, thou shalt always feel dejected, disquieted, discontented and be intolerable to thyself, if not also to others; and what is of greater consequence, thou wilt incur a great risk of being lost eternally.

It is certain, at all events, that the gate of perfection will be closed against thee, there being no other door by which thou canst enter save that of humility.

Strengthen thyself, therefore, with a holy ardour, so that nothing may be able to subdue thee. Lift up thine eyes on high and there behold Jesus Christ, Who, heavily laden with His cross, teaches thee the road of humility and patience, trodden already by so many saints, who are now reigning with Him in heaven.

Hearken how earnestly He calls upon thee to follow the same road taken by Himself and by all the faithful imitators of His virtues.

See how the holy angels all long for thy salvation; see how they implore thee to enter upon that narrow path, the only safe one, nay, the only one which leads to heaven, and which will conduct thee to those thrones of eternal glory left vacant through the pride of the rebel angels.

And dost thou not already hear the blessed triumphantly proclaiming throughout Paradise that by no other road have they come to the possession of that immense glory, than by that of humiliation and of suffering?

See how they rejoice, and how gladsome they are with thee for those first desires which thou hast conceived of imitating their example.

Fortify thyself, therefore, with might and courage to set about this grand work without further delay.

Recall to thy mind those most sacred vows thou madest in thy baptism, and tremble at the mere thought of violating the sanctity of the solemn promises which thou didst then make
to God.

Know, beyond everything else, that Jesus Christ expressly declared, that the "kingdom of heaven suffereth violence" Matt 11:12 Blessed art thou, yea, a thousand times blessed, if, convinced of this truth, thou makest it thy first endeavour to practise humility, that so thou mayest merit the reward of the eternal greatness of heaven.

LX.

In the last place, reflect that our divine Master exhorted His disciples to acknowledge themselves "unprofitable servants" even when they had fulfilled all the Commandments!
Luke 17:10

So shouldst thou also acknowledge thyself an unprofitable servant, even after having practised all the foregoing counsels with the utmost exactness; being firmly convinced that such is not due to thine own strength and merits, but indeed to the gratuitous goodness and infinite mercy of God.

Thank Him without ceasing, with all the love and outpouring of thy heart, for so great a blessing.

Finally, beseech Him every day to vouchsafe to preserve this priceless treasure within thee, even to that very moment when thy soul, released from every tie which keeps thee bound to creatures, shall be free to wing its flight to the bosom of its Creator, there to enjoy for all eternity the glory prepared for the humble.

Sermon of St Augustine

On the Fear of God and on True Humility
(De Tempore Serm. 212)

DAVID, the Royal Prophet and Psalmist, who, as the Scriptures testify, being a man after God's own heart, performed His every will; this holy Prophet, I say, dearly beloved brethren, in a certain passage pointeth out to us what it is that our Creator desireth and loveth, crying out in these words: — "Who is as the Lord our God, Who dwelleth on high, and looketh down upon the low things in heaven and in earth." Ps. 112:5

If, therefore, the Lord Most High, of Whose perfection and greatness there is no end, regardeth and welcometh humility in all His creatures — be they the most exalted or the most lowly, angels or men — how necessary, therefore, must it be that we should continually look to humility and practise it always in everything, in order thus to give pleasure to our Creator.

How great a virtue, then, true humility is, may be gathered easily from those words of our Saviour, Who, to condemn the pride of the Pharisees, saith: — "Everyone that exalteth himself shall be humbled, and he that humbleth himself shall be exalted." Luke 14:11

It is only by the steps of humility that the heights of heaven can be reached, for not by means of pride do we mount to God on high, but in truth by humility, according to that which is written: — "God resisteth the proud, and giveth grace to the humble!" James 4:6 And it is written in the Psalms: — "The Lord is high and looketh on the low, and the high He knoweth afar off"Ps. 137:6 Here the high signify the proud. He looketh upon the low to exalt them, and knoweth the high afar off that is the proud, to cast them down. Let us learn humility in order to enable us to approach the Lord, as He Himself saith in the Gospel: — Learn of Me, because I am meek and humble of heart, and you shall find rest to your souls." Matt 11:29 By pride the once admirable and angelic creature was cast down headlong from heaven, and by the humility of God human nature ascended thither. Beautiful, even in the sight of men, is the practice of humility, as Solomon declareth: — Where pride is, there also shall be reproach, but where humility is, there also is wisdom." Prov. 11:2 Again, another wise man saith: — "The greater thou art, the more humble thyself in all things, and thou shall find grace before God." Eccles. 3:20 And God Himself saith by the mouth of His prophet: "To whom shall I have respect but to him that is poor and little and of contrite heart, and that trembleth at my words!" Isaias 66:2

In one who is not humble and meek the grace of the

Holy Spirit can never dwell. God humbled Himself in order to save us. Let man blush to be proud. As profoundly as the heart abaseth itself in humility, so high does it rise in perfection: for he who is humble shall be exalted in glory. The first degree of humility is, to hearken humbly to the words of truth, to keep them in memory, to practise them willingly. Truth, certainly, ever fleeth from a mind which is not humble. The less thou art in thine own estimation the greater wilt thou be in the sight of God. But the proud man, the more illustrious he appears to be to the world, the more contemptible will he be before God. He who practiseth all virtues, but with no humility, is like a man who carries dust before the wind. Furthermore, the Scripture crieth out: — "And why dost thou exalt thyself, dust and ashes!" Eccles 10:9 Whilst the wind of pride carries away and scatters all that thou imaginest thyself to have amassed by fasts and alms.

Be well on thy guard, O man, lest thou make a boast of thy virtue; for thou shalt not thyself be thine own judge, but Another, before Whom, strive to keep thyself lowly of heart, in order that He may exalt thee in the day of recompense. Descend, therefore, in order to ascend. Humble thyself that thou mayest be exalted, lest having exalted thyself thou shouldst be humbled. For he who is unsightly in his own eyes, is beautiful before God. He who is displeasing to himself, is pleasing unto God. Be therefore little in thine own eyes, so as to be great in the eyes of God; for the more vile thou art in thine own estimation, the more precious shalt thou be in the sight of God. In the highest honours, have the deepest humility. Honour deriveth its greatest glory from the virtue of humility.

But this virtue of humility no man can have without the fear of God, because the one cannot exist without the other.

Now with regard to the effect of the fear of God, hearken to me, my brethren: — "The beginning of wisdom is the fear of the Lord" Ps. 110:9 The fear of the presence of God is a great preservative against sin. He who perfectly feareth God, taketh great care to avoid sin. " With him who feareth the Lord, it shall be well in the latter end" Eccles. 1:13 and his recompense shall endure for ever. If a person be ashamed to transgress before men, how much more commendable and requisite, then, is it that he should be ashamed to commit iniquity in the sight of God, Who looketh not only to the deed, but, likewise, to the heart. Those who fear God with a holy fear seek the things that are pleasing to Him. There is the fear of children and there is the fear of servants. Servants fear their masters for the dread of punishment, but children fear for the love of their father. If we be children of God, let us fear Him for the sweetness of charity, not out of the bitterness of fear. The wise man in all his actions feareth God, because he knoweth it is impossible to hide from His presence, according to the words of the Psalmist when addressing God: — "Whither shall I go from Thy spirit, or whither shall I flee from Thy face." Ps. 138:7 to which is added, in another place: — "From the east even unto the west there is no hiding-place for him who fleeth from God." He who feareth the Lord will accept His doctrine, and he who shall be careful to keep His commandments, shall find everlasting benediction. "The soul of him that feareth the Lord is blessed," Eccles. 34:7 he abideth secure from the temptations of the Evil One. "Blessed is the man who is always fearful," Prov 28:14 and to whom it is given to have ever before his eyes the fear of God. He who feareth the Lord turneth aside from the crooked way and directeth his steps in the path of virtue. "The fear of the Lord driveth out sin," Eccles. 1:27 and induceth virtue. The fear of God rendereth man careful and anxious not to sin. But where there is no fear of God there is dissoluteness of life. He who feareth not God in prosperity, let him at least fear Him in adversity, and let him fly for succour to Him Who scourgeth and healeth, for: — "Blessed is the man that feareth the Lord, and who endeavours with all the desires of his heart to keep His commandments." Ps. 111:1 The fear of God driveth out the fear of hell, because it maketh a man avoid sin and multiply his works of justice. After this, he will arrive at that fear which, being founded upon love, is called — "holy, enduring for ever and ever." Ps. 18:10 Thus, therefore, brethren, thus let us fear God that we may love Him, for perfect charity casteth out servile fear, and by this means we shall acquire abundant security and the plenitude of every good. Wherefore the Royal Prophet saith: — "Fear the Lord all ye His saints, for there is no want to them that fear Him. The rich have wanted and suffered hunger, but they that seek the Lord shall not be deprived of any good." Ps. 33:10, 11. I implore you, therefore, dearly beloved, to keep in view the fear of God; ever in your minds, to strive at all cost not to be unmindful of His precepts, and to consider seriously, that whereas he who feareth God and keepeth His commandments entereth into life everlasting, he who despiseth Him and rejecteth His precepts, will go into everlasting torments.

Once more, I beseech you, to nourish interiorly within your hearts true humility, and by its unfeigned practice, to instill it into your neighbours, so that they also, being edified by your good example, may glorify God, and in union with you, strive to obtain an eternal reward in heaven, through the help and grace of our Lord Jesus Christ, Who liveth and reigneth for ever and ever. Amen.

VARIOUS THOUGHTS ON HUMILITY.

KNOW, ye humble, that our Redeemer "humbled Himself, becoming obedient unto death." Phil 2:8 Know, ye proud, that of your Chief it is written, "He is king over all the children of pride." Job 41:25 The beginning of our ruin, then, was the pride of the devil, and the cause of our redemption was the humility of God.

For our enemy being created like all other things, wished to appear to be exalted above all, but our Redeemer, the greatest above all things, deigned to become the lowliest of all. Therefore, tell the humble, whilst they abase themselves they rise to the imitation of God, and tell the proud, whilst they exalt themselves, they sink down to the imitation of the apostate angel. Is there anything, therefore, more despicable than pride, which, whilst it exalts itself, recedes from the height of true greatness? Or is there anything more glorious than humility, which, whilst it stoops to the lowest depths is united to the Most High, its Creator? — St. Gregory the Great (Past, Par, iii. Adm, xviii.)

II.

In nothing can the two virtues of humility and charity be separated. And so inseparable is their connection, that he who is established in the one, is of necessity master of the other. For as humility is a part of charity, so is charity a part of humility. And if we carefully reflect on those works which the Apostle terms fruitless, and of no profit without charity, 1 Cor. 13:1-3. we shall find that these very same works are sterile if they be devoid of true humility. And of a verity, what fruit can knowledge produce united with conceit; or faith with human glory; or almsgiving with ostentation; or martyrdom with pride? Wherefore, since humility and charity both tend alike to the destruction of pride, what has been said of the one may be also applied to the other. — St. Ambrose (Epist. Libr, x. ad Demetriadem)

III.

Charity is preserved by means of humility, for there is nothing which destroys it so quickly as pride. Hence the Lord did not say: "Take up My yoke upon you and learn of Me," to raise the dead, who had been in the grave four days; to cast out evil spirits from demoniacs; to heal diseases and work other similar miracles; but He did say: — "Take up My yoke upon you and learn of Me, because I am meek and humble of hearth." Matt 11:29 These miracles, indeed, are indications of spiritual things, but to be meek and humble is the preservative of charity. — St. Augustine (In exposit. Epist. ad Galatas),

IV.

He who knoweth that he is dust and ashes, and into dust must soon return, will never proudly exalt himself: and he who has pondered upon the eternity of God, and reflects upon that short space, or, so to speak, point of space, which constitutes human life, will ever keep death before his eyes, and be humble and lowly. For this corruptible body weigheth down the soul, and our hearts, entangled with so many things, become depressed by this earthly tabernacle. Wherefore, let us say in all humility: — "Lord, my heart is not exalted, nor are my eyes lofty; neither have I walked in great matters, nor in wonderful things above me." Ps. 130:1

All true humility, then, is to be sought, not so much in words as in the mind, so that in the inner-most conviction of our souls, we should acknowledge ourselves to be nothing; nor ought we ever to imagine ourselves either to know or to understand anything, or to be anything at all. — St Jerome (In exposit. Epist. ad Ephes, cap, iv.)

V.

My son, have a care above all things of humility, for this, of all virtues, is the most sublime, and the ladder whereby to reach the summit of perfection.

Good resolutions are not carried into effect save by humility, and the labours of many years are brought to nothing through pride. The humble man is like unto God, and carries Him within the temple of His heart, but the proud man, in being odious to God, bears resemblance to the devil. Although the humble man may appear outwardly loathsome and contemptible, yet he is glorious in his virtues, and not withstanding the loud display of state and dignity the proud man may make in sight of the world, yet his works quickly betray him as a man of no worth. His pride is detected by his gait and every movement, and his levity becomes apparent even in his words. He ever craves after the praises of men, and destitute as he is of all virtues, he goes about pretending to be full of them to the overflow. He cannot bear to be subjected to anyone, but ever aims at pre-eminence above others, and does all in his power to advance to a higher rank. That which he cannot obtain by merit, he endeavours to usurp by ambition. He walks about swelled with conceit, like a bag full of wind, and in all he does shows so much fickleness, that one might take him for a ship, which deprived of its captain, has become the sport of the billows. The humble man, on the contrary, shuns every earthly honour, reckons himself as the least of men, and though to look at, he would be taken to be of little importance, yet he stands eminently high before God. When he has fulfilled all that was commanded him he affirms that he has done nothing, and is most solicitous to conceal every virtue of his soul. But the Lord brings to light all his works, and proclaims them far and wide. He discovers his marvellous deeds to the world. He will exalt him and make him glorious, and in the hour of his prayer, grant him all he shall ask. — St. Basil the Great (Admon, ad Fil. Spir.)

VI.

The poor in spirit are the humble of heart that is to say, those are called poor in spirit who hold themselves in low estimation. On the contrary, by the rich in spirit is understood the proud, who have a high opinion of themselves, and do not fulfill the commandment of Jesus Christ, which declares that: — "Unless you become as little children, you cannot enter into the kingdom of heaven" Matt 18:3 for whosoever has already become as a little child, is poor in spirit, and he who is poor in spirit has indeed become as a little child. And although, according to the testimony of Jesus Christ and of the Apostle, Matt 22:39 love is the fulfilment of the law, yet the nurse of love is humility, and the mother of hatred is pride.

Therefore, humility is the beginning of all good, and the origin of every evil is pride. — St Jobn Chrysostom (Parall. Lib. iii. cap, Ixxxiv.).

VII.

Behold wherein consists the foundation of humility: Rom 13:10 to reckon one's self a sinner, and to believe that one has done nothing well in the sight of God. Now, behold wherein consists the practice of humility: in the love of silence; in not comparing one's self with others; in not contradicting; in walking in subjection; in observing custody of the eyes; in picturing death to the mind; in abhorring falsehoods; in fleeing unnecessary and idle talk; in not opposing elders; in not being wedded to one's own opinion; in suffering injuries; in hating slothfulness; in always finding occupation, and being ever watchful. O brother, do thou endeavour to practise diligently these precepts in order that thy soul may not become a den of most vicious affections.

Labour at each one of them with alacrity, so as not to render void and unfruitful this brief course of thy life. — St. John Damascene (Parall Lib, iii. cap, Ixxxiv.).

VIII.

The true humility of the faithful soul lies in this: not to pride one's self upon anything; not to murmur against anyone; not to be ungrateful, nor complaining, nor querulous, but in all things to thank God and to praise Him, Whose works are either justice or mercy.

Hence, whatsoever may befall thee, always return thanks to the Lord. — St Anselm (Comm. in 1 Thess, cap. v.).

IX.

"I am the flower of the field and the lily of the valley" Cant 2:1 "The Just shall spring as the lily." Os. 14:6 Who else is just but the humble? Jesus, Lord as He was, bowed beneath the hands of His servant, the Baptist; and to the Baptist, standing awe stricken at His majesty, He exclaimed: — "Suffer it to be so now, for so it becometh us to fulfill all Justice," Matt 3:15 thereby evidently showing, that He placed the fulfilment of all justice in humility. The just man, therefore, is a humble man, the just man is the valley. If we also be found humble, we likewise shall spring up as the lily, and we shall flower for all eternity before the Lord.

Will not Jesus, indeed, then show Himself to be more especially the lily of the valley, when "He will reform the body of our lowness, made like to the body of His glory!" Phil. 3:21 The Apostle docs not say our body, but the body of our lowness, in order to point out that the humble will be illuminated by and clothed in that wonderful and ever enduring candour of the lily. This is what was to be said on the protest made by the Spouse of the sacred Canticles, that He was the Flower of the field and Lily of the valley. — St. Bernard (Super Cantica Ser, xlvii.)

X.

True humility makes no display of being such, and does not speak much of itself, because it not only desires to hide all other virtues, but more especially seeks to conceal itself. Were it lawful to make use of falsehood, deceit, and bad example, it would perform acts of arrogance and haughtiness so as to remain concealed under these subterfuges, and there to live unknown and secure. Hearken, then, to my advice: either let us never speak at all about humility, or if we do, let what we express outwardly be prompted by a true interior feeling. Never let us cast down our eyes without also humbling our hearts. Let us not appear desirous of being amongst the lowest, unless we really wish it. The truly humble man prefers others to say of him that he is a wretch, that he is of no account, that he is a good-for-nothing, rather than say so of himself. At all events, when he hears others speaking ill of him, he will by no means contradict them, but agree with them readily, because believing it all true himself, he is glad also to see others share his opinion. — St. Francis of Sales (Phil. Par. vii. cap, v.),

XI.

When thou art offered an insult, bear it with patience, and increase thy love towards him who shows thee contempt. This is the touchstone for ascertaining whether or no a man be humble and holy. If he yields to resentment, although he should work miracles, put him down as a tottering reed. Father Balthesar Alvarez used to say, that the time of humiliations was the time for heaping up treasures of merit. Thou wilt gain more by accepting an insult with patience, than by fasting ten days on bread and water. The humiliations which are self-imposed are good, but to accept the humiliations which we receive from others is far more profitable, because in these latter there is much less of self, and more of God. Hence, there is much greater merit if we know how to bear them patiently. But to what good can a Christian pretend if he cannot bear an insult for the sake of God? What contempt has Jesus Christ not suffered for us, — blows, derisions, scourgings, spittings in the face! Ah! If we had true love for Jesus Christ, not only would we not resent affronts, but even be delighted at finding ourselves despised as He Himself was despised. — St. Alphonsus Liguori (Oper. Spirit).

XII.

Oftentimes it is very profitable for the keeping us in greater humility that others know and reprehend our faults. When a man humbles himself for his defects he then easily appeases others, and quickly senses those that are angry with him.

The humble man God protects and delivers; the humble man He loves and comforts; to the humble He inclines Himself; to the humble He gives grace, and after he has been depressed raises him to glory. To the humble He reveals His secrets, and sweetly draws and invites him to Himself. The humble man having received reproaches maintains himself well enough in peace, because he is fixed in God and not in the world.

Never think that thou hast made any progress till thou look upon thyself as inferior to all (De Imit. Lib. ii. cap. 2)

XIII.

It is the common opinion of theologians that he who has a greater degree of charity will enjoy in a higher degree the light of heavenly glory.

This glory will be given only to the humble of heart, because true charity stoops to lowly things that it may ascend to things that are lofty. But why dost thou grow proud in the midst of earthly pomp, O dust and ashes, thou mass of rottenness and food of worms! If thou wouldst be abashed and ashamed of thyself, obtain a clear knowledge of thyself. The root of all evil is pride; that of all good is charity.

But thou wilt not be able to implant charity, until thou hast first pulled up pride by the roots. How to uproot it will be taught thee by charity. Charity alone knows how to resist the spirit of pride. Thou wilt resist the spirit of pride if thou hidest thy virtues, and layest bare thy defects. Be, therefore, very watchful and pay special attention to this, that the vice of pride consists chiefly in thy unwillingness to tolerate from others any reproach for those faults of which thou art ever ready to accuse thyself — Cardinal Bona (De Art Div, Am. cap, xix.)

XIV.

"If any man thinketh himself to be something, whereas he is nothing, he deceiveth himself" Gal. 6:3 Consider that if this saying, which the Apostle proposes for thy meditation, were well understood, it would put an end to all vain glory. How is it that so many get prouder from day to day? "The pride of them that hate thee ascendeth continually" Ps. 73:23 Because from day to day they become more blinded in the knowledge of themselves. They think within themselves, that of themselves they are something, whereas in truth they are absolutely nothing. Hearken, therefore, to that general declaration of the Apostle, which applies to all alike: If anyone, be he who he may, thinketh himself to be something, he does not say something great — no! But simply, something — if anyone thinketh himself to be something whereas he is nothing, he deceiveth himself. This, therefore, is the sublime truth that ought at last to convince thee, that of thyself thou art nothing — Nihil es. And why? Because thou of thyself hast nothing except sin, which is the supreme nothing. Everything that thou hast outside of sin is ah of God. The deepening of one's knowledge of this truth is the way to arrive at true humility; for although the essence of humility consists in the lowly submission of the will, yet the standard by which the will fixes the degree of its greater or less self-abasement, comes only from the intellect — Fr Paul Segneri (Mann, dell. An. xi. Agost).

XV.

When thou art praised and honoured by others, unite thyself to the contempts, the derisions, the insults suffered by the Son of God. Take it for granted that a soul truly humble finds as much humiliation in honours, as it does in the midst of contempt It acts like the bee, which gathers its honey no less from the dew that falls upon the absynth, as from that which drops upon the rose. — St. Vincent De Paul.

XVI.

My children, be humble: be lowly. —
St Philip Neri

PRAYER.

To implore the grace of devotion and of humility.

O Lord, my God, Thou art all my good, and who am I that I should dare speak to Thee? I am Thy most poor servant and a wretched little worm, much poorer and more contemptible than I can conceive or dare express. Yet remember, O Lord, that I am nothing, I have nothing, and can do nothing. Thou alone art good, just, and holy: Thou canst do all things. Thou givest all things. Thou fillest all things, leaving only the sinner empty. Remember Thy tender mercies, and fill my heart with Thy grace. Thou wilt not have Thy works to be empty. How can I support myself in this wretched life, unless Thy mercy and grace strengthen me? Turn not Thy face from me, delay not Thy visitation, withdraw not Thy comfort, lest my soul become as earth without water to Thee. O Lord, teach me to do Thy will, teach me to converse worthily and humbly in Thy sight: for Thou art my wisdom. Who knowest me in truth, and didst know me before the world was made, and before I was born into the world. — (Imitation iii. cap, 3).

Made in the USA
Middletown, DE
11 June 2023